A TRUE BOOK™

The Sense of Sight

ELLEN WEISS

Children's Press®
An Imprint of Scholastic Inc.
New York   Toronto   London   Auckland   Sydney
Mexico City   New Delhi   Hong Kong
Danbury, Connecticut

Content Consultant
Lawrence J. Cheskin, M.D.
John Hopkins Bloomberg School of Public Health
Baltimore, MD

Library of Congress Cataloging-in-Publication Data

Weiss, Ellen.
  The Sense of Sight / by Ellen Weiss.
      p. cm. -- (A true book)
  Includes index.
    ISBN-13: 978-0-531-16871-4 (lib. bdg.)
          978-0-531-21833-4 (pbk.)
    ISBN-10: 0-531-16871-9 (lib. bdg.)
          0-531-21833-3 (pbk.)

1. Vision--Juvenile literature. I. Title.

  QP475.7. W45 2008
  612.8'4--dc22   2007048085

Produced by Weldon Owen Education Inc.

Find the Truth!

Everything you are about to read is true *except* for one of the sentences on this page.

Which one is **TRUE**?

T or F There is a tiny brain inside your eye.

T or F Dark-colored eyes offer more protection from bright light than do light-colored ones.

Find the answers in this book.

Contents

THE BIG TRUTH!

An ostrich's eye is bigger than its brain.

4 Life Without Sight

How does vitamin A help you see? 35

5 Stand Guard!

Why must you never look directly at the sun? . . . 41

5

Without light,
you would not
be able to see.

6

CHAPTER 1

Sight and Light

Sight begins with light. Right now, light is hitting this page and bouncing off the page into your eyes. Inside your eyes, these light rays are turned into information. The information travels to your brain. Your brain turns it into an image that has color, shape, depth, and movement. All this happens so quickly that you are not aware of any delay between looking at something and seeing it.

You do not actually see an object. What you see is a pattern of light reflected off it.

7

The Eye We See

The purpose of the eye is to **focus** light to enable us to see. All parts of the eye play a role in this.

The black circle in the middle of your eye is an opening that lets in light. It is called the pupil. The size of the pupil changes as the amount of light changes.

Around the pupil is the iris. This is the colored part of the eye. The iris contains two muscles that control the size of the pupil. By regulating the amount of light that enters the eye, these muscles help make vision possible.

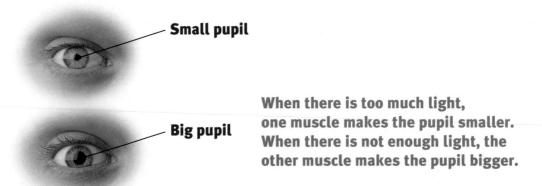

Small pupil

Big pupil

When there is too much light, one muscle makes the pupil smaller. When there is not enough light, the other muscle makes the pupil bigger.

8

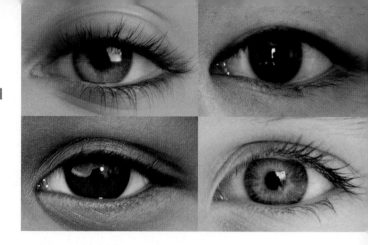

Light-colored eyes are slightly more sensitive to light than dark-colored eyes because they have less protective pigment.

Eyes come in different colors and shapes that we inherit from our parents. The iris color comes from melanin (MEL-uhn-in). Melanin is a dark **pigment** that also gives hair and skin their color. Dark-colored irises contain a lot of melanin close to the surface. Light-colored irises contain very little melanin. Melanin absorbs light, helping to protect the eyes.

 Emotions, such as anger or fear, can also make the pupil change size.

9

Focus on Light

Your eye is actually hollow, but it is filled with a jelly-like fluid. Light entering your eye must first cross the cornea. This tough, clear dome of transparent cells protects the iris and pupil from particles and damaging light rays. The cornea also bends the light rays toward the center. This bending is the first step in focusing the light. The rays then pass through the pupil and the eye's lens.

Object

Light rays

The curve of the surface of the lens changes according to the light. In this way, light rays are bent at the angle that allows for the sharpest focus.

The lens is a clear, flexible disc. The light rays cross each other after they pass through it. Finally, the rays land on the **retina**. There they form an image. However, because the rays crossed each other, the image is upside down!

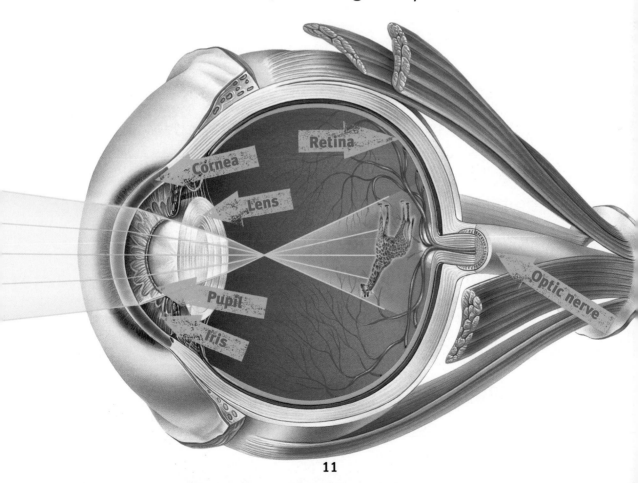

Retina

Cornea

Lens

Pupil

Iris

Optic nerve

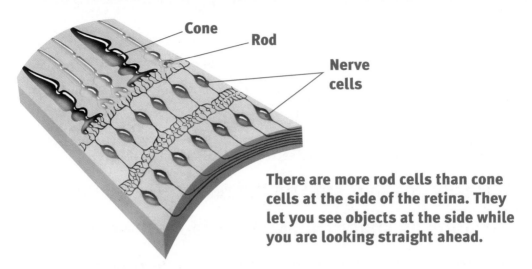

Cone

Rod

Nerve cells

There are more rod cells than cone cells at the side of the retina. They let you see objects at the side while you are looking straight ahead.

Sight Cells

The retina is about the size of a bottle cap. It is something like a movie screen. As in a movie, a visual image is projected onto the retina by way of light. In your retina, there are about 126 million photoreceptor, or light-receiving, cells. These cells change light energy into electrical energy. That is the kind of energy used by the **nervous system** to transfer information. There are two kinds of photoreceptor cells, called rods and cones. Rods detect shades of black, white, and gray. Cones detect color and sharp detail.

12

Cone cells need more light to function than rod cells. That's why it can be hard to see colors at night.

Your Blind Spot

Behind the retina is the **optic** nerve. It sends the information from your eye to your brain. The tiny spot on your retina where your optic nerve leaves your eye is called your blind spot. When an image lands on that part of your retina, you cannot see it. There are no cones or rods there, so it can't respond to light.

Find Your Blind Spot

Hold this page at arm's length. Close your left eye and focus your right eye on the X. Now bring the page closer to your face. Does the dot disappear at one point? Yes, it does. That's because it's in your blind spot.

13

Sea stars have an eye at the end of each tentacle. The eyes can sense light and dark, but cannot see.

14

CHAPTER 2

Working Together

Whenever you see something, you have your eyes and brain to thank. They work together to make sight happen. In fact, your eyes are like a door connecting the visible world with the visual centers of the brain. Animals without backbones do not have that connection. Their eyes developed from a part of their skin. These eyes simply let the animal know when and where there is light.

A hermit crab can extend its eyes outside its shell, and pull them back in for protection.

15

In the Blink of an Eye

When an image lands on the retina, electrical energy sends the information along the optic nerve to the brain. On the way, the fibers of the optic nerve cross paths. The light that enters the right side of each eye is handled on the right side of the brain, and vice versa. It is because the brain combines these two images that we are able to see **three-dimensional** images.

The information goes first to the **thalamus**, in the middle of the brain. The thalamus sorts the information and sends it to the visual cortex, at the back of the brain.

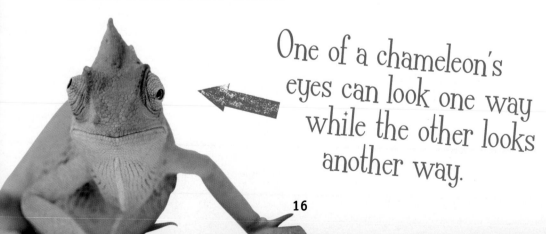

One of a chameleon's eyes can look one way while the other looks another way.

16

The Eye-Brain Connection

The brain is so important to our sight that if the visual centers in a person's brain are destroyed, the person will become blind even if the eyes are in perfect condition.

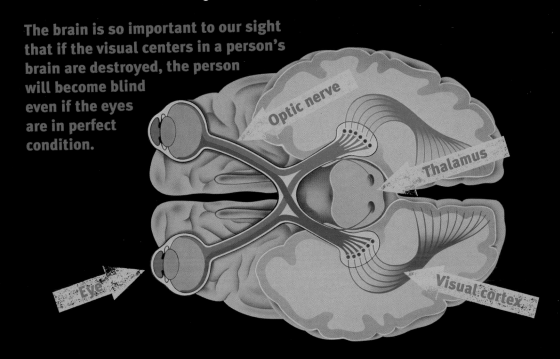

Optic nerve

Thalamus

Eye

Visual cortex

The visual cortex is where the brain makes sense of the information sent from your eyes. In a fraction of a second, the upside-down image on your retina becomes the right-side-up image you see. Scientists believe that the image isn't actually flipped. Rather, when we are babies, our brains learn to let us see the image the right way up.

17

Now You See It ... Now You Still See It

Have you ever noticed that the spokes of a moving bicycle wheel appear as a blur? This effect is caused by something called persistence of vision. Scientists think that, as you see something, your brain hangs onto the image briefly. In this way, successive images "overlap" and appear continuous. In medium light, an image may be held for about one tenth of a second.

Check Your Persistence of Vision

Count slowly to 20 while looking at the green bird's eye. Then look at the cage. You should be able to see a shadowy pale pink bird. Do the same with the red bird. You should be able to see a shadowy bluish bird. Why are the shadowy birds a different color? See page 48 for the answer.

18

Humans process about 60 images a second in daylight and 10 at night.

It is persistence of vision that keeps the world from going black every time you blink. It also makes movies and cartoons possible. They are made of thousands of still pictures. The pictures move very fast— from 10 to 30 pictures every second. Persistence of vision helps us see these images as a continuous moving picture.

When we watch a movie, we are not aware that we are actually looking at still pictures joined together.

19

That's Deep

One of the things your eyes and brain need to figure out is how far away things are, and how thick objects are. This is called depth perception. It gives you a three-dimensional view of the world even though the image on the retina is flat. Without depth perception, simple actions, such as walking down stairs or riding a bike, would be very difficult.

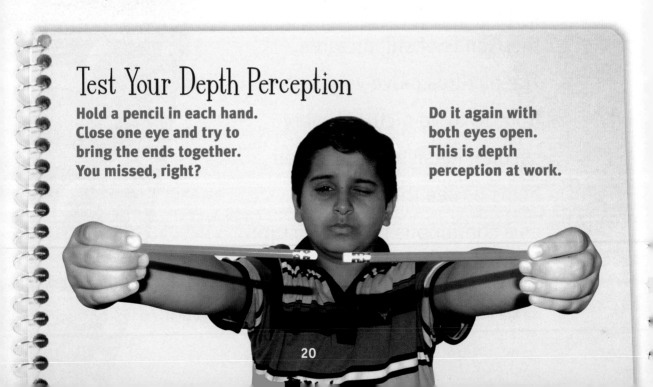

Test Your Depth Perception

Hold a pencil in each hand. Close one eye and try to bring the ends together. You missed, right?

Do it again with both eyes open. This is depth perception at work.

20

We are not born with depth perception. It develops during the first six months of life.

Both eyes are needed for depth perception to work properly. Your eyes are a short distance apart, so they see two slightly different flat images. Your brain uses information about the differences to create one three-dimensional image. Scientists believe that only mammals have depth perception.

Without depth perception, it would be very hard to judge when to swing a bat in order to hit a ball.

21

20/20 Vision

E

H N

D F N

P T X Z

U Z D T F

D F N P T H

P H U N T D Z

N P X T Z F H

Have you ever heard someone say that he or she has 20/20 vision? The numbers are a comparison of a person's eyesight with a standard based on "normal" eyesight. If you can see from 20 feet (6 meters) what most people can see from that distance, then your vision is 20/20. If your vision is 20/50, you must be at 20 feet to see what most people can see at 50 feet (15 meters). If your vision is 20/10, you can see at 20 feet what most people can see only at 10 feet (3 meters).

Watchmakers work with tiny pieces of machinery. They often use a magnifying eyepiece called a loupe to help them see.

Eyes at Work

Would you like to use your eyes all day for a living? Fire spotters, lifeguards, astronomers, lighting designers, artists, medical researchers, and technicians are some people who do. Often they rely on devices that aid natural vision. Binoculars, microscopes, telescopes, and X-rays all help people see what they need to see.

A Machine That Sees

Have you ever thought about how a camera works? As long ago as the civilizations of ancient Greece and ancient China, people thought about a machine based on the human eye.

A camera is much like an eye. In both an eye and a camera, an adjustable opening lets in light. Both have a lens that captures and focuses the light. In a camera, the lens moves forward or backward to focus. In your eye, muscles change the shape of the lens to find the best focus.

A dragonfly's eye has about 10,000 lenses.

24

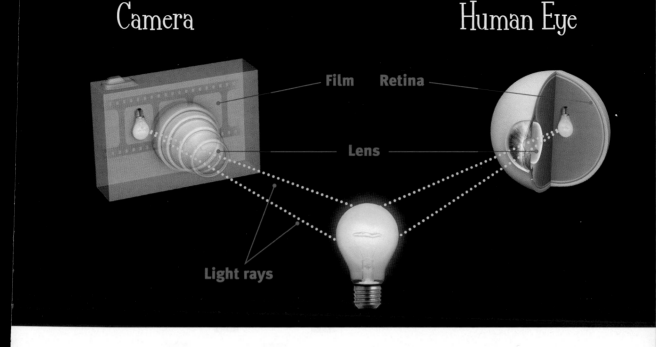

Camera   Human Eye

Film   Retina

Lens

Light rays

In an eye, the light travels to the retina. It is converted to electrical energy, which the brain translates into an image. In a film camera, the film acts like a retina. When the film is processed, the chemicals on the film reveal the places where the light fell. In a digital camera, the light detector converts light to electrical pulses. This electrical information is stored in the camera's memory, the "brain" of the camera.

3. Which rows are straight? Which rows are on an angle? The answers may surprise you.

4. What do you see in this picture?

5. Can you figure out where each pipe starts?

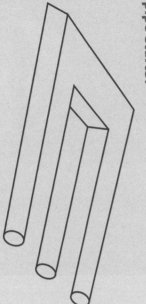

6. Which line is longer?

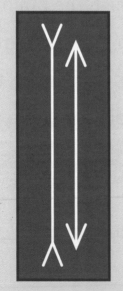

Answers on page 48.

THE BIG TRUTH!

Optical Illusions

Your brain works hard to make sense of the information your eyes send it. But sometimes things can be tricky, even for your brilliant brain. Your brain is used to getting visual information in certain ways. When things are not as expected, your brain can get mixed up. It sees what it expects to see.

1. The bar in the center of this box is shaded from light green to dark green. Or is it? Cover the background and take another look.

2. Look at the circles. Are they moving?

27

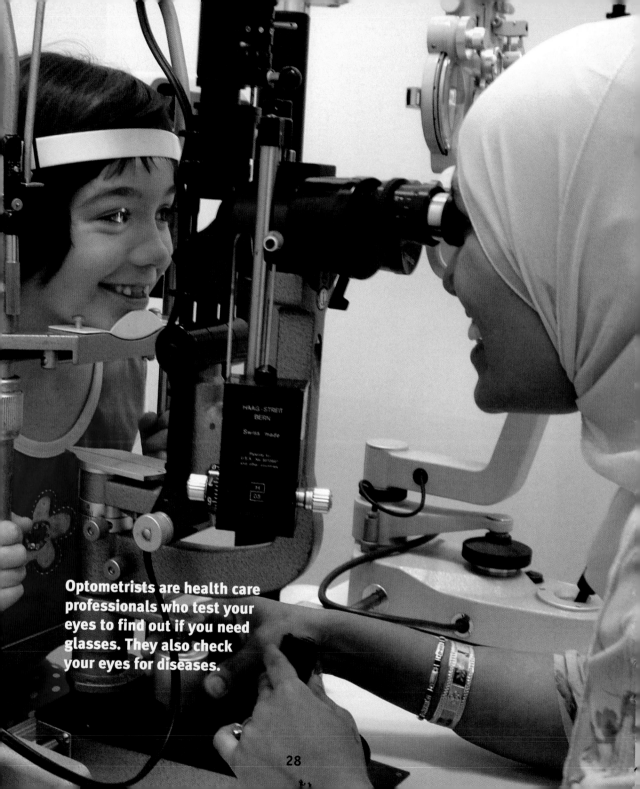

Optometrists are health care professionals who test your eyes to find out if you need glasses. They also check your eyes for diseases.

CHAPTER 3

When Things Go Wrong

Most kids who need glasses are nearsighted. That means they have trouble seeing things that are far away. As adults age, they often become farsighted. That means they have trouble focusing on things that are close.

 By looking into your eyes, doctors can find out about your health as well as about your eyes.

Shape and Sight

After light rays pass through the lens of the eye, they meet and cross paths. The place where this happens is called the focal point.

In perfect vision, the focal point is positioned so that a clear image is projected on the retina. However, if the eyeball is too deep or too shallow, the focal point is affected. This can cause nearsightedness or farsightedness.

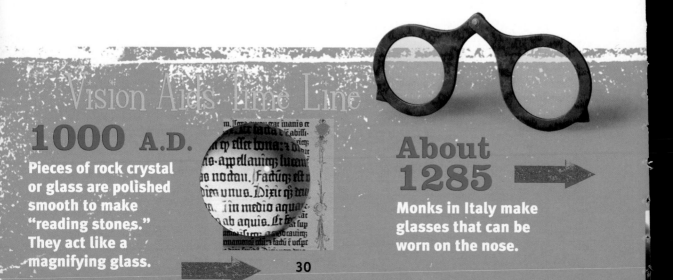

Vision Aids Time Line

1000 A.D.
Pieces of rock crystal or glass are polished smooth to make "reading stones." They act like a magnifying glass.

About 1285
Monks in Italy make glasses that can be worn on the nose.

30

In nearsightedness, the focal point is too far from the retina. As a result, the image falls short of the retina. In farsightedness, the focal point is too close to the retina, or beyond it. Therefore, no image can form inside the eye.

Nearsightedness and farsightedness can be treated with glasses or contact lenses. The manufactured lens corrects the problem so that a clear image lands on the retina.

1784
Benjamin Franklin invents bifocals. These are glasses with two parts. One is for nearsightedness and one is for farsightedness.

1888
German biologist Adolf Fick invents the first contact lenses.

Solving the Problem

The corrective lenses used in glasses or contact lenses make the image hit the retina where it's supposed to. Lenses to correct nearsightedness are thinner in the middle than at the edge. Lenses to correct farsightedness are thicker in the middle than at the edges.

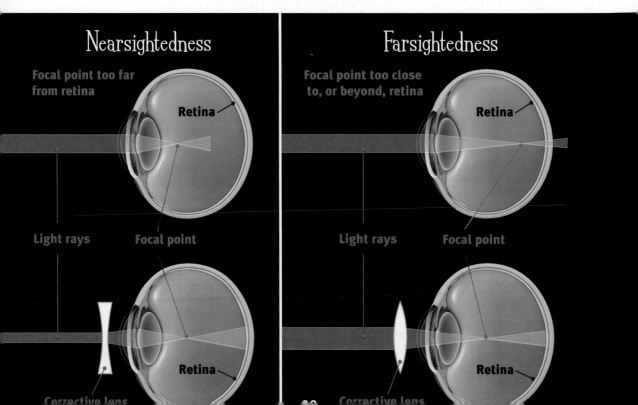

Nearsightedness

Focal point too far from retina

Retina

Light rays

Focal point

Retina

Corrective lens

Farsightedness

Focal point too close to, or beyond, retina

Retina

Light rays

Focal point

Retina

Corrective lens

What Color Is That?

Color blindness is something you are born with. People with color blindness aren't blind to color. However, they often find it hard to tell apart shades of red and green, or of blue and yellow. Sometimes they don't see colors the same way other people do. About one in 12 males is color blind. Fewer than one in 200 females is color blind.

Although it is mostly males who are color blind, color blindness is passed down through the females in a family.

If you can't see the numeral 3 in this circle, you may be color blind. Ask an optometrist.

33

Guide dogs help people who cannot see. The first guide dogs were trained in Paris in about 1780.

34

CHAPTER 4

Life Without Sight

"Max, forward," the young woman says. Holding his harness, she waits for the pull. Then she steps forward. All around, she hears noise—traffic, people talking, shoes clattering. She can't see anything, but Max will keep her safe. Suddenly, he nudges her to the left. She hears the whoosh of a bicycle just where she was standing. Life without sight is full of challenges.

Today, miniature horses are being trained as guides for visually impaired people.

Causes and Cures

Some people are visually impaired from birth. Blindness can be inherited. It can also result from an illness or injury. About 75 percent of people who are legally blind can see something, such as light, outlines, or shadows.

Many of the conditions that may lead to blindness are related to aging. Cataracts make the lens of the eye cloudy. Glaucoma (glaw-KOH-muh) is caused when the liquid in the eyes doesn't drain properly and pressure builds up. If it is detected early, it can usually be controlled with treatment.

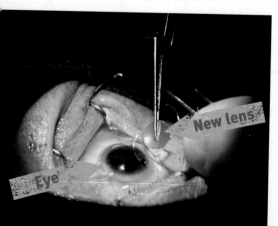

New lens

Eye

Today, cataracts need not cause blindness. The lens of the eye can be replaced with a plastic lens.

36

Every year, about half a million children go blind because of **malnutrition**. They do not get enough vitamin A from their food.

In some places, trachoma and river blindness cause many people to go blind. Both diseases can be treated with antibiotics. However, getting the medicine to the people is difficult.

People with **diabetes** risk blindness from high levels of sugar in the blood. With early treatment, though, blindness can be prevented.

Some campaigns against blindness have been very successful. Measles is one cause of blindness. However, it has been wiped out in most of the world by a **vaccine**.

Rod cells need vitamin A to work properly. Vitamin A helps you see in the dark.

Carrots are rich in vitamin A.

37

A Helping Hand

A number of inventions have made it easier for people who are blind or visually impaired to connect with the world around them.

Braille is a system of writing. People "read" Braille by running their fingers over a page that has a different pattern of raised dots for each letter. Today, visually impaired people have access to Braille computers and printers.

A robotic assistant has been developed to help people who are blind find what they need in stores. Radio identification tags are attached to products. The machine has a sensor that identifies products by the tags.

38

Vision Without Sight

Sight is important, but people can live good lives without it. Visually impaired people do all kinds of things and work at all kinds of jobs. They are scientists, factory workers, musicians, lawyers, teachers, car mechanics, and salespeople.

People who are missing one sense often make up for the lack of it by using their other senses more. In fact, the visual cortex in people who are blind seems to "rewire" itself to receive input from other senses. People who are visually impaired often have excellent senses of touch, hearing, and smell.

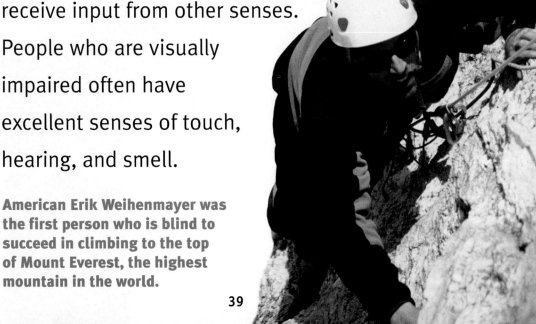

American Erik Weihenmayer was the first person who is blind to succeed in climbing to the top of Mount Everest, the highest mountain in the world.

39

You must use special glasses to look at a solar eclipse.

40

CHAPTER 5

Stand Guard!

Your eyes are very good at protecting themselves, but you have to protect them too. Too much bright light can permanently harm your eyes. That is why you mustn't ever look directly at the sun, even during a **solar eclipse**. It's also a good idea to wear sunglasses on bright days.

There is no pain when the retina is being burned. By the time symptoms appear, the eyes have been permanently damaged.

41

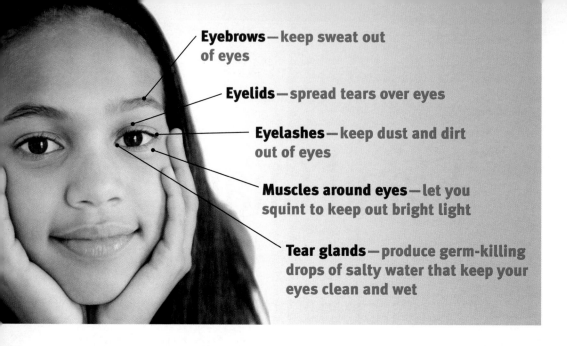

Eyebrows—keep sweat out of eyes

Eyelids—spread tears over eyes

Eyelashes—keep dust and dirt out of eyes

Muscles around eyes—let you squint to keep out bright light

Tear glands—produce germ-killing drops of salty water that keep your eyes clean and wet

Make Them Last a Lifetime

Your sight is precious. You want it to last for your whole life. If you are reading, make sure that you have enough light. If you are at the computer or watching TV, give your eyes a rest now and then. Point the hole in spray cans away from yourself. If you are doing chemistry experiments at school or playing sports, use the correct eye protection.

By taking care of your eyes, you may prevent damage and keep them healthy. ★

True Statistics

Number of times you blink in a minute:
Between six and 30

Time your eyes are closed every day, just from blinking: About 30 minutes

Number of fibers in human optic nerve:
1,200,000

Number of fibers in cat optic nerve: 119,000

Number of muscles that move each eye around:
Six

Time it takes for a rod cell to change light energy to electricity: One-quadrillionth of a second

Speed at which light travels: About 186,282 miles (299,792 kilometers) a second

Did you find the truth?

(F) There is a tiny brain inside your eye.

(T) Dark-colored eyes offer more protection from bright light than do light-colored ones.

43

Resources

Books

Cobb, Vicki. *Open Your Eyes: Discover Your Sense of Sight*. Brookfield, CT: Millbrook Press, 2002.

Cole, Joanna and Degen, Bruce. *The Magic School Bus Explores the Senses*. New York: Scholastic, 2001.

Murphy, Patricia J. *Sight* (A True Book). New York: Children's Press, 2003.

Silverstein, Dr. Alvin and Virginia, and Silverstein Nunn, Laura. *Can You See the Chalkboard?* (My Health). Danbury, CT: Franklin Watts, 2001.

Silverstein, Dr. Alvin and Virginia, and Silverstein Nunn, Laura. *Seeing* (Senses and Sensors). Brookfield, CT: Twenty-First Century Books, 2001.

Simon, Seymour. *Eyes and Ears*. New York: HarperCollins, 2003.

Taylor-Butler, Christine. *The Nervous System*. (A True Book: Health and the Human Body). Danbury, CT: Children's Press, 2008.

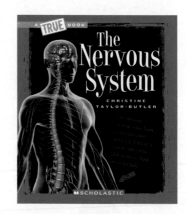

Organizations and Web Sites

Neuroscience for Kids
http://faculty.washington.edu/chudler/neurok.html
Learn all kinds of things about how your brain and senses work, and play games to test your own reactions.

Optical Illusions
www.michaelbach.de/ot/
These incredible illusions will keep you busy for days.

Your Sense of Sight
http://library.thinkquest.org/3750/sight/sight.html
Read more about your sense of sight, then learn about your other four senses.

Places to Visit

The Exploratorium: Museum of Science, Art, and Human Perception
Palace of Fine Arts
3601 Lyon Street
San Francisco, CA 94123
(415) 561 0360
www.exploratorium.edu
Hands-on exhibits are designed to inspire your curiosity about science.

Museum of Science
Science Park
222 Jersey City Boulevard,
Boston, MA 02114
(617) 723 2500
www.mos.org/
Find out what's inside your body at the Human Body Connection exhibition.

Important Words

diabetes (dye-uh-BEE-teez) – a disease in which there is too much sugar in the blood

focus – to adjust the lens of an eye or a camera in order to see an object properly

malnutrition – a condition caused by not having enough to eat or eating the wrong kind of food

nervous system – a system in the body that includes the brain, spinal cord, and nerves

optic – related to eyes or eyesight

pigment – a natural substance that gives color to another substance or material

retina (RET-uhn-uh) – the lining at the back of the eyeball that is sensitive to light and sends images to the brain

solar eclipse – a blocking out of some, or all, of the sun's light. It occurs when the moon comes between the sun and Earth.

thalamus (THAL-uh-muhss) – the part of the brain that transfers information relating to the senses

three-dimensional – having length, width, and height; having depth

vaccine (vak-SEEN) – a medicine that prepares the body to fight a future infection

46

Index

Page numbers in **bold** indicate illustrations.

47

About the Author

Ellen Weiss went to Oberlin College and Columbia University. She has worn glasses since she was eight years old. Ellen has used her eyes in the writing of more than 200 books, both fiction and nonfiction, for children of all ages. She has also written songs and created videos. Her work has won a Grammy Award, a Parents' Choice Award, and three Children's Choice Awards.

Ellen and her husband, Mel Friedman, live in New York. They often write books together. The Disney Channel adapted one of their books, *The Poof Point*, for a T.V. movie. They have a daughter who uses her ears in her career as a violinist.

Answers

Page 18:

When you look at the green bird, your cone cells become accustomed to the green color. Then, when you look at the cage, you see the white light without the green. White light without green light is the pinkish color you see. The same thing happens when you look at the red bird. White light without red is the blue/green color you see.

Pages 26–27:

1. The whole bar is the same shade.
2. The circles are not moving.
3. All the rows are straight.
4. You may see a vase. You may see two faces. You may see both.
5. Try drawing this yourself. You may still find it hard to figure out!
6. The lines are the same length.